1. Aberdeen
2. Aberdeenshire
3. Arran & Ayrshire

12. Fife, R...
13. Glasgow
14. Inverness
15. Islay, Jura, Colonsay & Oronsay
16. The Isle of Skye

17. Lanarkshire
18. Lochaber
19. Loch Lomond, Cowal & Bute
20. Loch Ness
21. The Lothians
22. Moray
23. Mull & Iona
24. Orkney
25. Orkney in Wartime
26. The Outer Hebrides
27. The City of Perth
28. Highland Perthshire
29. Ross & Cromarty
30. Royal Deeside
31. Shetland
32. Stirling & The Trossachs

The remaining four books, Caledonia, Distinguished Distilleries, Scotland's Mountains and Scotland's Wildlife feature locations throughout the country so are not included in the above list.

D0582221

PICTURING SCOTLAND

ROYAL DEESIDE

COLIN NUTT
Author and photographer

2   The Royal Bridge over the River Dee at Ballater. This is the fourth bridge here, the previous three having all been swept away.

ROYAL DEESIDE

Welcome to Royal Deeside!

Even in a country so blessed with dramatic landscapes, some areas stand out as exceptional. Even by Scotland's high standards, the slice of Aberdeenshire that lines the course of the River Dee has a reputation for scenic splendour that many believe sets it apart. There are so many different forms of landscape in Scotland that it is impossible, foolish even, to credit any one part of the country as the 'best' or the most beautiful; and yet a few corners of the land have that magic ingredient that imbues them with some facet of character or combination of features that marks them out as special.

Perhaps it is that Deeside tells a complete story, takes one on a journey (quite literally) from mountain spring to waiting sea, revealing the ages and stages of a process that so dynamically shapes the land and holds the fortunes of its inhabitants in its watery hand. As rivers go, it does not rank high in terms of length – 85 miles – but few if any others start in such dramatic or remote surroundings. The Wells of Dee are 1220m/4000ft up in the Cairngorm Mountains, a short distance from which the infant burn falls over a near-vertical corrie edge and crashes down into the Lairig Ghru, that huge glacial trench that cuts right through the Cairngorms. Up here in this tundra world rare plants grow and rare birds live, their arctic abode becoming less and less what they need as the climate warms. Yet, for now,

Deeside begins here: 1220m/4000ft up in the Cairngorm Mountains near the summit of Braeriach, 5
even in June the headwaters tumble through snow at the top of the Falls of Dee.

moss campion and mountain saxifrage, the ptarmigan and the dotterel can still be seen.

As the Dee matures into a larger river, fed by countless tributaries born of other mountain crannies, it descends into a glen of many colours and textures: heather and pine, rock and bracken, a different world into which humankind has roamed for millennia. Archaeological evidence shows that people have settled on the banks of the River Dee since Mesolithic times: as the ice receded and flora and fauna returned, people soon followed. The oldest known settlement is at Birkwood where Mesolithic micro flints over seven thousand years old have been found. Around 2000BC tribes of Picts and Celts arrived in the area and in 300AD the Romans came. So many episodes in Scotland's history have taken place here. The first church in Scotland dedicated to St Andrew was built near where Braemar Castle stands today; and speaking of Braemar, Malcolm Canmore camped near where the village now stands while on his way to confront Macbeth. The battle took place further down Deeside at Lumphanan in 1057 and Macbeth was defeated.

Most famously of all, midway along Deeside in the shadow of the mountain called Lochnagar,

6   The ptarmigan, seen here in winter plumage, is a rare bird of the high Cairngorms.

stands Balmoral Castle, summer home of the Royal Family. Queen Victoria and Prince Albert's holiday at the Balmoral Estate in 1848 marked the beginning of a life-long love affair with the region and put the 'Royal' into Royal Deeside. Their decision to buy and develop Balmoral Castle had a profound effect on the development of the area. In Banchory, Aboyne, Ballater and Braemar most of the important buildings were built in the Victorian era. Her influence can still be experienced in the Victorian Heritage Trail.

This book follows the river from source to sea, thus making the 85-mile journey from west to east, with occasional detours to north and south to take in places of interest that are within Royal Deeside's sphere of influence. So now, whether you are a resident or a visitor, let this pictorial journey remind you of, or prepare you for, the best that this glorious river-world has to show.

Moss campion flowering on the Cairngorms plateau at around 1220m/4000ft.

8   This grand vista shows the mountain setting into which the Dee flows. Taken from the slopes of Braeriach, we look south down the Lairig Ghru, the great glacial valley that carves its way through

the Cairngorms. The peak at the end of the ridge on the left is Carn a' Mhaim (1037m/3402ft), while on the other side of the glacial trench are the Devil's Point (1004m/3294ft) and Cairn Toul.

10 Left: the summit of Braeriach (1296m/4252ft), not far from the source of the Dee.
Right: the dotterel is a scarce summer visitor to mountain areas in Scotland, mainly the Cairngorms.

This picture follows the one on p.5 in charting the next stage in the progress of the Dee as it 11
tumbles through the Garbh Corrie between Braeriach and Sgor an Lochain Uaine (1258m/4127ft).

12 The rugged end of Deeside: from a gully near the summit of Braeriach, here is the view across the uppermost part of the Dee's course to Cairn Toul (1291m/4236ft) rising above Lochain Uaine.

A few miles into its journey and having turned east, the river reaches the Linn ('gorge pool') of Dee, **13** with winter volume of water rushing through. Queen Victoria opened the bridge in 1857.

14 The Dee is joined from the north by Quoich Water, pictured here at the Linn of Quoich with the Punchbowl – a curious bowl-shaped depression in the rock – visible to the left of the icy rapids.

From near the Linn of Quoich, an easterly scene looking towards Braemar, in which the hill to the 15
right of centre (Creag Choinnich) provides the viewpoint for the picture on p.21.

16 A north-westerly view from near Inverey of the high Cairngorms at their magnificent winter best. On the left is the Devil's Point and on the right Cairn Toul.

Mar Lodge. The huge Mar Lodge Estate, owned by the National Trust for Scotland, is recognised **17** as one of the most important nature conservation landscapes in the British Isles.

18 Amongst the wildlife to be seen is the very rare capercaillie, the most impressive of the grouse family; and red squirrels, plentiful for now but under threat from encroaching grey squirrels.

From the upper Deeside road near Inverey, an impressive view of Beinn a' Bhuird (1197m/3927ft), **19** several miles to the north. Snow always makes the mountains look more spectacular.

20 The River Dee meanders through pine forest at Inverey west of Braemar, its character now considerably different from the tumbling mountain stream seen back on p.11.

The village of Braemar is in the highest parish in Scotland. This westerly view from Creag Choinnich **21** shows that it is located where Glen Clunie (coming in on the left) joins Deeside.

22　Glen Clunie leads to Glen Shee, one of Scotland's five ski resorts.

Braemar itself is a very attractive and interesting place. Here, the bridge over Clunie Water is on the left and the War Memorial is on the right. 23

24 The mountains north of Braemar are great walking territory. This panorama in upper Glen Quoich shows Beinn a' Bhuird left and centre, including the A' Chioch crags seen on p.19. To the right is

Carn Eas, the southern part of Ben Avon (1171m/3842ft), of which more later. This picture fits in between the views on pages 33 and 34.

26 Braemar is most famous for the annual Braemar Gathering, always held on the first Saturday in September. Attended by the Royal Family, it is a magnificent pageant of marching bands and

highland games, including Tossing the Caber, above. Among other events are the shot-put, throwing the hammer, races and highland dancing.

28 Creag Choinnich provides a good vantage point to look down on Braemar Castle which John Erskine, Earl of Mar (1558-1634), started building in 1628. It is open to visitors in summer.

Again from Creag Choinnich, this is Invercauld House, at the heart of the Invercauld Estate. **29**
It occupies approximately 200 square miles of spectacular Deeside scenery.

30 East of Braemar and looking north-west, an archetypal scene that shows Deeside at its spring best: green tones are revived, the river is well filled but not in spate and snow remains on the high slopes.

The old Brig o' Dee between Braemar and Crathie, looking pristine, having just been restored. **31**
Above is the summit of Lochnagar which will be seen in more detail later.

32 It may be fanciful, but the heather in Deeside seems to possess an extra vibrancy; perhaps, in this image, it has something to do with the early morning light at Keiloch, east of Braemar.

No, this picture should not be turned 90°: the tree is growing horizontally! It is in Glen Slugain, **33** seen on the early stages of the long walk through Invercauld Estate from Keiloch to Ben Avon.

34 Further along this mountain hike the waters of Glas Allt Mor ('big green water') cascade down
through a series of falls, one of which is seen here. From here the going gets steeper, en route to

the Sneck, where these weather-shaped rocks could almost pass for Neolithic standing stones.
The Sneck is the dip, or 'bealach', between Beinn a' Bhuird and Ben Avon.

36 A stiff pull up from the Sneck brings walkers to the Ben Avon plateau, from where a final mile or so leads to the c.30m/100ft summit tor named Leabaidh an Daimh Buidh, meaning 'bed of the yellow stag'.

Near the top of the ridge on the northern edge of Deeside, the expansive view into Glen Gairn opens **37** up. The Gairn is a tributary of the Dee, the confluence of the two rivers being a few miles further east.

38 Gairnshiel Bridge crosses the Gairn burn. This handsome structure was built in 1751. The Gairn meets the Dee just west of Ballater.

Another look at Glen Gairn, this time from the north at a point on the road in the distance on p.37. **39**
This view is therefore looking south towards Deeside.

40 For all the summer splendour of the heathery scene in the previous picture, this upland landscape is arguably more impressive in the depths of winter. This is Glen Gairn from the north. The next stage

of the journey takes us back over the hills on the extreme right to return to Deeside near Balmoral.

42 There have been several centres of worship in Crathie going back to the 6th century. Queen Victoria laid the foundation stone of today's Crathie Kirk and it was completed and dedicated in 1895.

Just across the Dee from Crathie is the Royal Lochnagar Distillery. It was granted a Royal Warrant of Appointment by Queen Victoria in 1848. Guided tours are available to visitors.

44 Balmoral Castle, the ultimate symbol of what put the 'Royal' into Deeside. It has been a royal castle for over 160 years. Queen Victoria and Prince Albert signed the lease in February 1848.

They soon began negotiations to buy and in June 1852 Prince Albert concluded the purchase. Plans were **45** then drawn up for a larger castle to replace the original. The castle of today was completed in 1856.

46 The Old Royal Station in the bonny village of Ballater saw a century of service from 1866 to 1966. As the nearest station to Balmoral, it saw much Royal patronage in its heyday. Tragically, it burnt

down in 2015 but has been re-built in as faithful a copy of the original as possible. However, as this 47 book goes to press, the red paint seen above is being replaced by light green.

48 A recent addition to the collection is this superb reconstruction of Queen Victoria's railway carriage.

The stunning interior of the carriage, where a soundtrack recreates an imagined conversation **49** anticipating their return to Balmoral.

50 Many businesses in Ballater have Royal Warrants which permit them to carry the relevant coats of arms on their premises. Queen Elizabeth II's coat of arms is on the left.

Silhouetted in the last light of an autumn evening, Glenmuick Parish Church dominates the green in 51 the middle of the village.

52 Left: the flower beds around the War Memorial front this view which shows Craigendarroch rising to the west of the village. Right: looking across Ballater's village green to a cottage door.

And so to the 'White Mounth', the most easterly part of the Cairngorm Mountains. **53**
Its focal point is Lochnagar, seen here from the north side of Deeside, looking south.

54 Climbing Lochnagar mountain entails walking around a corrie rim, where this jumble of rocks overhangs the view down into Lochnagar, the corrie lochan from which the mountain takes its name.

Loch Muick, the largest loch in the Cairngorms, lies at the head of Glen Muick, south of Lochnagar. **55**
On a cloudless day the water really is this colour. Broad Cairn (998m/3274ft) towers above.

56 Beautiful Glen Muick runs south-west from Ballater, climbing into the White Mounth, an outlier of the main Cairngorms range. The Lochnagar massif dominates the horizon. The high point towards

the left is Cuidhe Crom, one of the subsidiary tops of Lochnagar. The actual summit is over to the right but hidden in this view (see p.59).

58 Looking east from near the summit, the south-Deeside hills stretch away into the distance. The peak in the middle distance with an obvious path going up it is Meikle Pap.

And finally, walkers reach Cac Carn Beag, the little tor that forms the very top of Lochnagar at **59** 1155m/3789ft. This area is part of the huge Balmoral Estate which extends to just over 50,000 acres.

60 The view down from Lochnagar really captures the essence of Deeside. Invercauld House and Brig o' Dee can both be seen – compare this picture with those on pages 29 and 31.

Similarly, from near the summit of Broad Cairn (compare with p.55), we now see Loch Muick from **61** on high, just as evening shadows are engulfing the end of the loch.

62 Left: a quaint survivor at Cambus o' May – this old AA call box has been beautifully restored.
Right: a typical Deeside Christmas-card scene.

The Dee is in one of its more placid stretches at Cambus o' May, where this elegant suspension **63** bridge is a product of the Edwardian era.

64 Tucked away to the north of Cambus o' May is the well-hidden but spectacular Burn o' Vat.
The approach path seems to end at a wall of rock, but then a narrow entrance tunnel appears (left)

that leads into this deep, water-gouged bowl, a product of melt-water at the end of the Ice Age. The right-hand picture opposite shows the entry from inside while, above, an idea can be gained of its size.

66 About three miles east of Cambus o' May, Loch Kinord in the Muir of Dinnet Nature Reserve makes a fine sight to the north of the A93. A way-marked trail goes around the loch, starting at Burn o'Vat.

Spring comes to the pretty Deeside village of Aboyne, founded in 1671 by the first Earl of Aboyne. **67**
The Huntly Arms Hotel looks out onto the village green.

68 The seasons roll by and autumn leaves frame the gates that lead to the Green of Charlestown, home of the village's Highland Games since 1867.

Aboyne-Dinnet Parish Church on a winter afternoon. It is situated at the opposite end of the **69** Green of Charlestown from the view opposite.

70 Glen Tanar runs south-west from Aboyne. This is the Water of Tanar near the top of the glen, looking south to Mount Keen (939m/3081ft).

Winter can last a long time on Deeside. This beautiful scene at Potarch was recorded in early March. 71

72 A few miles north of Deeside is Tomnaverie recumbent stone circle, built c.2500BC. This type of monument is peculiar to north-east Scotland, 'recumbent' referring to the stone placed horizontally

between two uprights – just left of centre. The purpose of this arrangement is unclear, although here 73 the three stones frame the full moon around midsummer at the limit of its movement across the sky.

74 The Old Kirk, Kincardine O'Neil. Dedicated to St Mary, the church is thought to have been built around 1338. Despite renovations in 1799 and 1830 it was replaced by a new building in 1862.

A spectacular dawn over Torphins, a north Deeside village, with the Hill of Fare beyond. **75**

76 Of the hills to the south of Banchory, the tor-topped peak of Clachnaben (589m/1932ft) is the most dramatic. It is a rewarding climb and not too strenuous walk of about three hours.

And the reward is, of course, the views to be enjoyed, this being the northerly one towards Deeside. 77

78 Left: Banchory High Street showing West Parish Church and the Burnett Arms. Right upper: Burnett Arms Hotel sign with horn motif. Right lower: pestle and mortar above the chemist's door.

A lovely display of heathers at the Gordon Highlanders' Memorial in Banchory.

80 The Falls of Feugh are a short walk from the centre of Banchory. The footbridge is a
    popular place for spotting salmon leaping. This is the view downstream towards Banchory.

The main body of the falls is on the upstream side of the bridge. **81**
The burn is the Water of Dye, on its way to join the Dee.

82 Just east of Banchory, Crathes Castle, with its late 16th-century tower house and later additions. It runs an active programme of events and is a National Trust for Scotland property.

Crathes is famed for its wonderful Arts and Crafts gardens and here we see 83 a vibrant array of flowers in one of the greenhouses.

84 Summer colours in the herbaceous borders at Crathes Castle Gardens. In all, they cover 3.75 acres and are divided into eight square compartments each of which has a different character.

The Deeside Railway opened to traffic on 8th September 1853 and closed in 1966. A section has **85** been restored and trains run from Milton of Crathes to the outskirts of Banchory.

86 Deeside has a great wealth of castles. Here we see Drum Castle, with its 13th-century tower house, adjoining Jacobean mansion house and Victorian additions.

The tiny but delightful chapel that stands in the grounds of Drum Castle. **87**
It can still be used for weddings.

88 Nearing journey's end: the River Dee has completed most of its 85-mile course as it approaches Aberdeen. From Tolohill to the south-west of the city we see the river spanned by the Bridge of Dee.

Aberdeen, the Granite City, is Scotland's third largest with a population of approximately 210,000.

90 Near the city centre, the elegant Wellington suspension bridge of 1831 remains in use for pedestrians only, thus making it the most pleasant way to cross the Dee in Aberdeen.

Perhaps the most defining view of Aberdeen is this one, from Castlegate, **91** looking down Union Street with the Townhouse taking centre stage.

92 Down by the mouth of the Dee is Foot Dee ('Fittie'), the old fishing village district of the city. Many of the houses are built around traffic-free squares, making for an oasis of urban calm.

What's more, it is only a stone's throw from Fittie to Aberdeen's magnificent and extensive beach. **93**

94 This is the business-end of the Dee, full of craft of all description, many of which serve the oil industry. In the distance, Victoria Bridge marks the inner limit of the harbour.

Finally, a birds-eye view of Aberdeen harbour. Victoria Bridge can be seen towards the right, **95** beyond which Scotland's most regal river melts into the North Sea.

Published 2018 by Lyrical Scotland, an imprint of Lomond Books Ltd, Broxburn, EH52 5NF
www.lyricalscotland.com www.lomondbooks.com

Originated by Ness Publishing, 47 Academy Street, Elgin, Moray, IV30 1LR
(First published by Ness Publishing: 1st edition 2010, reprinted 2012, 2nd edition 2015)

Printed in China

All photographs © Colin and Eithne Nutt except pp.6 & 18 (left) © Mark Hicken; p.18 (right) © Charlie Phillips;
p.22 © Glenshee Ski Centre; p.26 © Braemar Gathering; p.43 © Diageo; p.44 courtesy of Balmoral Castle,
© Jim Henderson; pp. 62 (right), 70, 71 & 75 © Jim Henderson; p.95 © Scotavia Images.
Cover image © Colin Nutt, used by kind permission of Balmoral Estate.

Text © Colin Nutt
ISBN 978-1-78818-024-5

Front cover: Balmoral Castle; p.1: greenhouse flowers at Balmoral; p.4: marching at Braemar Gathering;
this page: winter woodland near Allanaquoich; back cover: River Dee at Inverey